The Precinct of Mut at South Karnak

The Precinct of Mut at South Karnak

An Archaeological Guide

Richard A. Fazzini
and Betsy M. Bryan

The American University in Cairo Press

Cairo   New York

First published in 2021 by
The American University in Cairo Press
113 Sharia Kasr el Aini, Cairo, Egypt
One Rockefeller Plaza, 10th floor, New York, NY 10020
www.aucpress.com

Dar el Kutub No. 19391/19
ISBN 978 977 416 973 1

Dar el Kutub Cataloging-in-Publication Data

Fazzini, Richard A.
        The Precinct of Mut at South Karnak: an Archeaological Guide, Richard A. Fazzini,
Betsy M. Bryan.— Cairo: The American University in Cairo Press, 2021.
        p.   cm.
        ISBN 978 977 416 973 1
        1.   Egypt, Antiquities
                I.   Bryan, Betsy M.
                932

1 2 3 4 5   25 24 23 22 21

Designed by Rafik Abousoliman
Printed in China

Table of Contents

Who Was Mut?

"Mistress of peace and of the war cry. Lady of heaven, queen of the gods—Great Mut. Creator. Protector. Lady of joy. Cobra of dread. The vigilant mistress of Karnak. Mighty ruler in her Theban Temple. She whose spirit exists because her temple endures. She whose temple and city will exist for millions of years."

Excerpts from a hymn in praise of Mut

Eye of Re Goddesses

Mut was an important deity with more than one primary identity. In the early New Kingdom, including during the reign of Hatshepsut (c. 1478/72–1458 BC), Mut's primary role at the temple of Isheru was as an "Eye of Re," one of a group of goddesses that were daughters of the sun god and could be both benign and dangerous. They included Sekhmet, Isis, Hathor, Bastet, Nekhbet, Wadjet, and others who could be both gentle cats and fierce lionesses. As the uraeus goddesses, perched on the sun god's forehead, they influenced the Nile floods and brought health or illnesses as the god determined. The cults of Eye of Re goddesses became vital to Egyptian life and rule.

By the reign of Amenhotep III (c. 1390–1353 BC), Mut's second role, as the consort of Amen, one of Egypt's most important gods, and the mother of the moon god, Khonsu, had become more prominent and is the guise in which she is perhaps best known. As the home both of Amen's consort and of the Eye of Re, her temple precinct in Thebes was an important religious center for almost two thousand years.

In her human form, Mut bore and preserved Egypt's kingship and, therefore, the king himself. Some kings, including Taharqa of the Twenty-fifth Dynasty, depicted themselves as the physical son of Amen and Mut. As lioness-headed Sekhmet ("The Powerful"), Mut was the fierce protector of Egypt, bringing defeat and death to its enemies and guaranteeing its annual renewal of life for the faithful. She could threaten Egypt, too, if the proper rituals were not performed to turn her into a gentle cat.

Stories of Sekhmet and the Eye of Re

There are two main myths about the Eye of Re. In the first, an aging Re becomes angry with humanity, which has become rebellious. He decides to destroy it, sending his Eye, Sekhmet, from his forehead to carry out the deed. Eventually the other gods convince Re to change his mind and call Sekhmet back, but she refuses. Re decides to trick her: he has a lake filled with beer dyed red and Sekhmet, convinced it is blood, consumes it all. Drunk on the beer, Sekhmet no longer wants to kill and returns to Re. In later periods, the Mut Temple, surrounded on three sides by a sacred lake called the Isheru that is specific to Eye of Re goddesses, represented the refuge in which Sekhmet was kept content and where she could bear her children in peace and safety.

In the second tale, Re and Sekhmet quarrel and she disappears to Nubia, refusing to return. Re sends Thoth (or other gods, depending on the version of the story) to convince her to come back. He finally succeeds, after many tricks and despite

Sekhmet's furious temper. On her return, she is greeted with celebrations and festivals throughout the country. The return of the distant goddess marked the return of the waters of the Nile at the start of the inundation and was celebrated through-out the country for centuries.

It was essential to keep the dangerous Eye of Re happy and contented to prevent her from unleashing death and destruc-tion on the country. The rituals to placate Mut and Sekhmet involved singing and dancing, feasting and drinking. A scene in the precinct's entrance (the Propylon) shows a Ptolemaic king and two priestesses playing music before the goddess in her two primary forms: queenly female and lioness-headed woman.

Sekhmet Statues

The site has long been famous for its statues of Sekhmet. Today many are housed in museums around the world. In the nineteenth century, the Sekhmets were what attracted the few photographers who visited the site. This photograph of the Mut Temple's First Court was taken by French photographer Henri Béchard sometime between 1869 and the 1880s.

Some have suggested there were originally 730 Sekhmet statues: two for each day of the year. They formed a "litany in stone" as one scholar called it, guaranteeing that the rituals to appease Sekhmet would continue even if there were no longer priests to perform the rites. Many scholars today believe that the statues originally stood in Amenhotep III's funerary temple on the west bank of the Nile, where more continue to be discovered. There is also the possibility that two separate sets of statues were created, one for each temple, and the probability that there were well over 730 is now a strong one.

Most of the statues show Sekhmet seated on a throne with an ankh held in her left hand and a sun disk on her head. The majority are slightly larger than life size (about two meters tall), but there are several on a larger scale, including the torso and lap of one enormous statue on the east side of the Mut Temple's Second Court. The head of this statue, found by Margaret Benson and Janet Gourlay in 1896 (see page 16), is now in the Luxor Museum.

The best-known Sekhmet is the one shown on page 7. She is over-life size and is crowned with a modius of cobras that would originally have supported a sun disk. Found by Benson and Gourlay, and restored in 2013 by Egyptian conservators taking part in an advanced conservation field school organized by the American Research Center in Egypt (ARCE), she sits regally in the Mut Temple's Second Court.

Standing statues of Sekhmet are less common, and the Mut Precinct itself boasts only a few, one of which was never finished and stands in front of Temple A's Second Pylon (left).

Another standing statue, also unfinished and missing its feet, (left) was found by the Supreme Council of Antiquities (SCA) in 2011 during the work to prepare the site to open to the public. It is now in storage at the Luxor Museum.

The Mut Precinct: Exploration

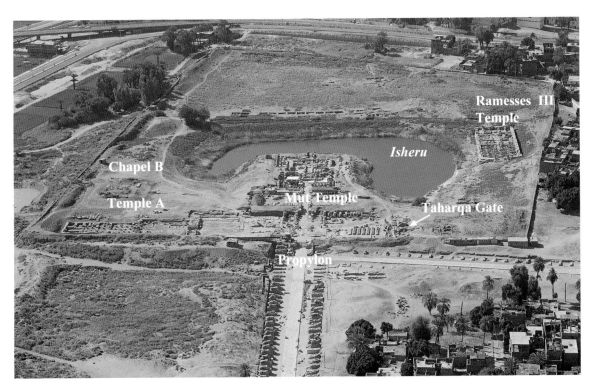

The Mut Precinct lies about one hundred meters south of the Amen Precinct at Karnak to which it is connected by an avenue of ram-headed sphinxes. The precinct's massive enclosure walls surround an area of approximately twenty acres. The site's main features are the Mut Temple, surrounded on three sides by the Isheru; a large temple in the northeast corner, referred to as Temple A because its ancient name is unknown for most of its history; a ruined building on a rise east of the Mut Temple referred to as Chapel B; a temple of Ramesses III southwest of the Mut Temple; a gateway built by King Taharqa of the Twenty-fifth Dynasty; and a number of smaller chapels.

It was probably under the Thirtieth Dynasty (381–343 BC) or the earliest Ptolemaic kings that the Precinct achieved its present size and its distinctive trapezoidal shape. The site as it now exists includes not only the buildings described, but a large area to the south of the Isheru that is still largely unexplored.

Tomb of Khabekhenet

The earliest representation of the precinct is a relief in the tomb of Khabekhenet at Deir el-Medineh (Theban Tomb 2), from the time of Ramesses II (c. 1279–1213 BC), complete with an avenue of ram sphinxes leading to the temple, a pylon gateway, two colossal statues in front of the temple, and the crescent-shaped sacred lake on which the barque of Mut sails from the west side (bottom) to the east. The details of the photograph have been outlined and highlighted to make them easier to see.

Early Exploration

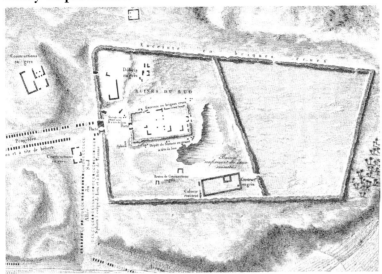

Napoleon took scientists as well as soldiers with him when he invaded Egypt in 1798. The *Description de l'Egypte* (1822) produced by the scientists was the first to include a detailed plan of the Mut Precinct, showing the site's main features: the Mut Temple and the Isheru (center), the temple of Ramesses III (lower right), and traces of Temple A (upper left).

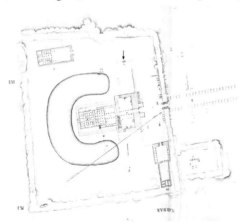

A few other explorers visited the site, including the Royal Prussian Expedition of 1842–45 led by Carl Richard Lepsius. The Lepsius map was the basis for this plan produced by Auguste Mariette, first director of antiquities in Egypt, for his 1875 book on Karnak. Mariette's book also included copies of important inscriptions, among them the ones in the Mut Temple's Montuemhat Crypt (see page 42). Note the small gateway (indicated by an arrow) in the upper right.

The first official excavations at the Mut Precinct were undertaken by two British women, Margaret Benson and Janet Gourlay, in 1895–97. They were the first women to direct excavations in Egypt. Little is known of Gourlay beyond the fact that she worked briefly with Flinders Petrie, but Benson was the daughter of the Archbishop of Canterbury and was considered brilliant by her contemporaries.

Although amateurs, they were able to call on the expertise of the leading scholars in the field and their book, *The Temple of Mut in Asher*, is on par with other reports of its time. The photograph on the right is from that book and shows excavations near the Contra-Temple (see page 43).

The next major work at the site took place in the 1920s under Maurice Pillet, director of the Egyptian Antiquities Organization, who cleared and mapped Temple A, in the process uncovering a second colossal statue of Amenhotep III (c. 1390–1353 BC) that had been usurped by Ramesses II and a large alabaster stela carved from a block of a shrine of Amenhotep II (c. 1426–1400 BC). It describes Ramesses' marriage to a Hittite princess.

Pillet also excavated the Temple of Ramesses III (c. 1187–1156 BC) southwest of the Isheru, and re-erected the two colossal statues of that king in front of the temple.

Modern Exploration

By the 1970s, most of the site was covered with rolling mounds of earth and debris, with only the major buildings partially visible. There had been no coherent exploration of the site as a whole, so it was unclear how the visible monuments related to each other.

In 1976, the Egyptian Antiquities Organization (now the Ministry of Tourism and Antiquities) granted the Brooklyn Museum permission to begin a systematic exploration of the northern half of the site and its monuments. The Detroit Institute of Arts assisted in this work from 1978 to 2010. Since 2001, Brooklyn has shared the site with a team from The Johns Hopkins University, which is concentrating on the Mut Temple itself and the area south of the sacred lake. The two teams work independently, but collaborate on projects where appropriate.

Both expeditions are grateful to the many senior officials of the Ministry of Tourism and Antiquities over the years who have granted permission to work at the site. They also acknowledge with thanks the cooperation and assistance of the Luxor office of the SCA and the many SCA inspectors with whom the expeditions have worked over the years.

The Early Mut Precinct

The relief in Khabekhenet's tomb suggests that the New Kingdom Mut Precinct consisted only of the Mut Temple and the Isheru. In 1983, the Brooklyn expedition discovered the gateway, shown in Mariette's plan of the site (page 15; indicated by arrow) but no longer visible. It was set into what was the west wall of the New Kingdom Mut Precinct. The Brooklyn team was able to trace the wall to its northwest corner, where it turns and runs on a line with the First Pylon of the Mut Temple, confirming that, indeed, the New Kingdom Mut Precinct was much smaller than it is today.

The gate's west (left) and east faces are inscribed for Thutmose III and Thutmose II (probably replacing an original Hatshepsut cartouche). The rectangular cutouts held blocks used to repair Amarna Period erasures of the name of Amen. The gate was fully excavated in 2001 by the Hopkins expedition.

On the west jambs are renewal inscriptions by Sety I (c. 1290–1279 BC) of the Nineteenth Dynasty, who restored the gate after the depredations of the Amarna Period.

On the south reveal, where it would have been hidden by the open door, there is a mostly erased graffito with the name of Hatshepsut, probably placed there by Senenmut, a powerful official under Hatshepsut. There is a small graffito of Ptah or Khonsu in a shrine at the east end of the south wall.

The Precinct Entrance

The Propylon is the massive stone gateway that guards the entrance to the precinct. It is inscribed for Ptolemy II (285–246 BC) and Ptolemy VI (180–164 BC, 163–145 BC). Like the gate in the Mut Temple's First Pylon, it contains scenes and texts relating to the cult of the goddess.

Between the Propylon and the Mut Temple

Along the enclosure wall east and west of the Propylon are rows of sphinxes and rams. When Brooklyn began its work in 1976, the sculptures were half-buried in dirt, and the first ram east of the entrance had been lying on its side for hundreds of years.

The Brooklyn team rebuilt the wall behind the eastern sphinxes and re-erected the fallen ram (below). The SCA restored the bases of three of the sphinxes west of the entrance, all of which were in worse condition than the ones to the east. Brooklyn cleared the earth from around them and built a mud brick wall behind the whole group to protect them from further damage.

The roadway from the Precinct entrance to the Mut Temple was paved with sandstone blocks that had decayed over the centuries. ARCE, with a grant from the United States Agency for International Development (USAID), repaired the roadway and installed signage (written by the Brooklyn and Hopkins expeditions) in 2012–13 in preparation for the 2014 opening of the site to the public. The structure in the foreground, behind the sign, is perhaps the foundation of an altar similar to the ones in the Amen Temple at Karnak. In the upper right is a series of platforms built to hold pieces of temple relief that cannot be put back in place.

The Horwedja Chapel

In 1978, the Brooklyn expedition found blocks from a small magical healing chapel reused in a late Ptolemaic or early Roman building in the Forecourt of Temple A (above).

The lintel to the chapel, along with other blocks from the Twenty-fifth to Twenty-sixth Dynasties had been reused to build the base of one of the sphinxes east of the Propylon (below left).

The tiny chapel (less than two meters square) probably stood originally in the front area of the Precinct and was dedicated by Horwedja, Great Seer of Heliopolis, a very important official in the Twenty-sixth Dynasty. This chapel, rebuilt by the Brooklyn Expedition, is one of the very few monuments to Horwedja in Upper Egypt.

Upside down lintel

The Mut Temple

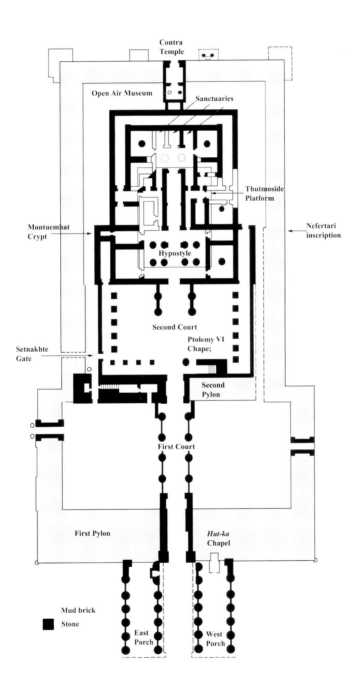

Contra
Temple

Open Air Museum

Sanctuaries

Thutmoside
Platform

Montuemhat
Crypt

Nefertari
inscription

Hypostyle

Second Court

Ptolemy VI
Chape;

Setnakhte
Gate

Second
Pylon

First Court

First Pylon

Hut-ka
Chapel

Mud brick

Stone

East
Porch

West
Porch

The Porches

When work began at the site in 1976, only the tops of two columns were visible in front of the Mut Temple's main entrance

(left), and they were clearly Ptolemaic in date. Yet in an inscription in the Mut Temple, Montuemhat, who rebuilt much of the Mut Precinct for Taharqa, said that he had built a colonnade of twenty-four columns here. When the Brooklyn team excavated the area, it uncovered two porches of twelve columns each, confirming Montuemhat's statement. The Ptolemies rebuilt the southern parts of the porches but seem to have been content simply to repair the rest of the columns.

East Porch   West Porch

At the south end of the porches are large Ptolemaic reliefs of the god Bes, often called a "dwarf god." With his mane-like hair and wrinkled forehead, it is possible that he is actually a lion, shown standing on his rear legs. Bes was one of the gods who enticed Sekhmet into returning to Egypt. More important, though, is his association with childbirth and the protection of pregnant women and newborn children. The cycle of birth and rebirth was an important part of Egyptian religion, particularly for mother goddesses such as Mut, Isis, and Hathor.

The Hut-ka Chapel of Nesptah

One important feature of the West Porch is a small chapel built into the mud brick pylon at its south end. It is a Hut-ka, a chapel dedicated to the *ka* (spirit/soul) of Montuemhat's son, Nesptah. Only two courses of the south wall were still in place, but the Brooklyn team found other blocks from the chapel in the same area. Like the Nitocris chapel in Temple A (page 50) and the Montuemhat Crypt in the Mut Temple (page 42), Nesptah's chapel is a rare example of a chapel for a private person in a major temple.

The Taharqa Rams

In 1979, at the north end of the East Porch, the Brooklyn expedition found a large granite head of a ram with a king below his chin, along with fragments of the king's body (left). The rest of the statue was a shapeless lump of granite. Stylistically the sculpture dates to the reign of Taharqa. It was eventually taken to Cairo to be displayed in the National Museum of Egyptian Civilization.

A second ram was found in 2001 at the north end of the West Porch. While headless, the sculpture preserves Taharqa's name on the base, confirming the date of the statue found in 1979. The Ptolemies seem to have left this pair of Kushite ram sphinxes in place when they refurbished the porches hundreds of years later. While there are many ram sphinxes of Taharqa in Sudan, the ones at Mut are rare examples of such sculptures in Egypt itself.

The First Pylon

In front of the pylon's west wing stand seven ram sphinxes that were probably moved there by Pinedjem I, a High Priest of Amen who became the first king of the Twenty-first Dynasty. At a later date, the three at the west end were moved off their bases and jammed together to create room to build a structure of unknown purpose where they once stood.

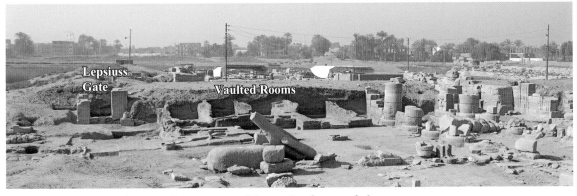

There is no evidence of rams or sphinxes in front of the east wing. Instead, a series of vaulted rooms was built against the pylon's face and other structures occupied the area between Temple A's First Pylon and the Mut Temple's East Porch. Coin evidence suggests that the earliest phases of these structures date to the Ptolemaic Period while the latest coins are from the reign of the Roman Emperor Antoninus Pius (AD 138–61). At the east end of the pylon is a small, uninscribed gateway that once led to the area east of the temple. Because it was first noted by Lepsius (see page 15), it is referred to as the "Lepsius Gate."

The entrance to the Mut Temple is a massive stone gateway in the First Pylon, which is built of mud brick. The walls of the gateway still bear Ramesside reliefs and inscriptions, but these were recarved in the Ptolemaic Period when Ptolemy VI remodeled and enlarged the gateway. The inscriptions on the gateway are important for the study of the goddess and her cult and were published by the Brooklyn expedition.

While the location of the temple's main entrance did not change over the centuries, the original Eighteenth Dynasty entrance was probably a smaller gate set into a mud brick wall rather than a massive pylon gateway.

The First Court
The Mut Temple's First Court is bounded on the north and south by the First Pylon and the Second Pylon. Both its east and west walls, of mud brick on top of baked brick (possibly an early Roman repair), are pierced by a stone gateway toward the south end of the court. The east gate opens onto the path to Chapel B (see page 55), while the west gate gives access to the area west of the temple.

The Second Court

The Second Court (below), whose walls bear reliefs carved by various Ramesside kings, fills the space between the Second Pylon and the stone rear half of the temple. On the north side of the Second Court, behind the large Sekhmet statue, is a small chapel built by Ptolemy VI. Square pillars that formed a peristyle line the sides of this court. Only the bases and fragments of the Hathor capitals remain.

A doorway in the east wall of the court, inscribed for Set-nakhte (c. 1190–1187 BC), founder of the Twentieth Dynasty, opens onto a corridor that runs from the Second Pylon around the rear of the temple.

Sekhmet Statues

These courts are notable primarily for their Sekhmet statues, most of which were partially buried when work began in the 1970s (above) and were threatened by rising groundwater that can destroy even diorite.

The Brooklyn and Hopkins expeditions have conserved all the statues at the site, placed them on bases that isolate them from groundwater, and built mud brick walls behind those in danger of being covered yet again in drifting earth.

In addition, the Egyptian conservators taking part in the conservation field school organized by ARCE, with a grant from USAID, conserved the large Sekhmet statue on the west side of the Second Court, and the over-life size statue of a king (Amenhotep III, usurped by Ramesses II) on the east side. These are two of the precinct's best-known monuments.

The Second Pylon

Like the Mut Temple's First Pylon, the Second Pylon was originally built entirely of mud brick.

This is unusual, as pylons are normally built of stone. The south face of the Second Pylon, which forms the north wall of the Second Court, was faced with stone in the Ramesside Period, and the east wing (top) was rebuilt in stone during the Ptolemaic Period. The job was never completed, however, and the blocks of that wing are still in their rough state. The west wing of the pylon was never changed at all. The Brooklyn expedition rebuilt this wing to a height of three meters to give an impression of what it would have looked like and to provide a backdrop for the Sekhmet statues before it.

The Rear of the Temple

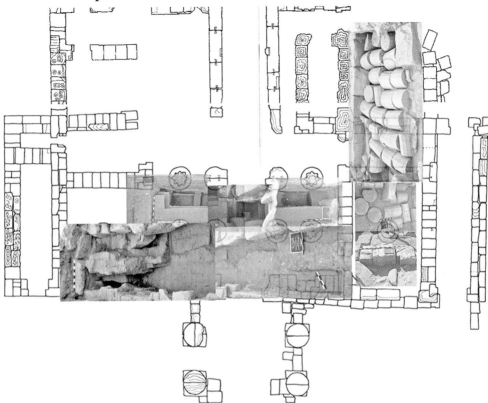

Although nothing remains visible, there may have been a temple to Mut here as early as the Middle Kingdom (c. 2055–1650 BC). In 2007, deep beneath the Thutmoside platform, the Hopkins team found a limestone fragment with the name of a king Senwosret and very likely the name Ish[eru], indicating a Middle Kingdom date for the site itself. The Hopkins expedition has also discovered what may be the foundations of a late Second Intermediate Period or early New Kingdom temple that had been covered by later construction. These earlier foundations are shown above, overlaid on a plan of the front section of the rear part of the temple.

The earliest standing monuments date to the reigns of Hatshepsut (c. 1478/72–1458 BC) and her

co-regent and successor Thutmose III (c. 1479–1425 BC). Among the limestone chips in a hole beside the remains of a small limestone chapel in the oldest part of the temple (page 35), the Brooklyn expedition uncovered a fragment of a cartouche containing part of Hatshepsut's name erased and replaced with the name of Thutmose III (left).

The Brooklyn Museum expedition uncovered the original Hatshepsut/Thutmose III temple platform, which is three courses deep and has very neatly beveled edges. Its location is shown on the Mut Temple plan on page 25. While little of the actual building remains, the guidelines that the Thutmoside builders etched into the surface of the platform show the position of the various chambers and elements, such as the torus moldings at the corners of the temple (below left).

The Hopkins expedition discovered that the original Hatshepsut/Thutmose III temple was redesigned and enlarged, probably by Thutmose III after Hatshepsut's death. Reused in the foundations of the north face of the west side of this temple were a number of decorated blocks from the earlier temple (now in the site's open air museum located at the rear of the east side of the temple).

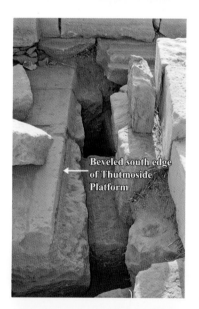

Beveled south edge of Thutmoside Platform ←

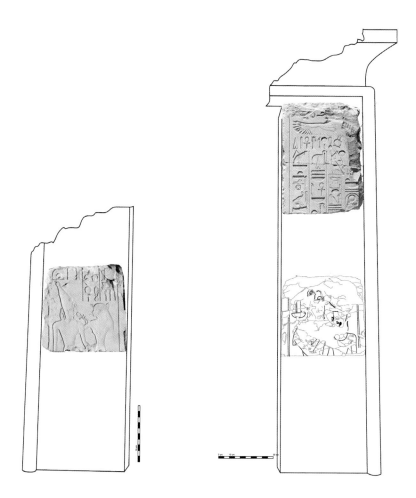

The Hopkins team dismantled and rebuilt this part of the foundations due to severe damage from intermittent groundwater. That resulted in the discovery of these aforementioned temple fragments, as well as limestone blocks from a doorway either to the temple itself or to a limestone shrine within the temple. Here is a reconstruction of the front of the gateway showing the position of two of the best-preserved blocks.

The foundations of the west side of the larger temple were even more interesting. They consisted of carefully laid column drums (visible in the photo on page 35) that had belonged to a "Porch of Drunkenness" built by Hatshepsut. Here a rite involving ritual drunkenness took place at certain times during the year. The Hopkins expedition restored the twelve-column porch, which now stands in an open area on the south side of the Second Court (below). This is not its original location, but it probably stood nearby.

Although the Ptolemaic inscriptions in the temple talk of singing, dancing, eating, and drinking to appease the goddess, drunkenness was not encouraged in ancient Egypt except in certain ritual acts meant to take people out of their normal selves in order to achieve union or communion with the gods.

The rear part of the temple, built entirely of stone, has mostly been destroyed down to the first or second courses and the bases of the columns.

It is approached through a small porch decorated with scenes probably commemorating the arrival of Nitocris I, daughter of King Psamtik I (c. 664–610 BC) of the Twenty-sixth Dynasty, to be installed as God's Wife of Amen, a position of great political and economic power, particularly in the Third Intermediate and Late Periods. The remaining blocks of these scenes (below) are now in the Egyptian Museum, Cairo.

South of the porch is a small Hypostyle Hall. While excavating this area, the Hopkins expedition uncovered a magnificent diorite statue of Queen Tiye, wife of Amenhotep III with an added inscription by the Twenty-first Dynasty queen Henuttawy, wife of Pinedjem I. The statue is now in the Egyptian Museum, Cairo.

Behind the Hypostyle Hall, in the center of the building, are the foundations of a long chamber called a "barque station" where Mut's sacred boat was stored when it was not being used in religious ceremonies.

At the rear of the building are the foundations of three shrines to Amen, Mut, and Khonsu. Beneath the central shrine, that of Mut, is a small crypt that has traces of an inscription naming King Taharqa of the Twenty-fifth Dynasty.

Sanctuaries

Crypt

The Later History of the Temple

The temple was enlarged again, probably during the reign of Amenhotep III, although nothing is left that positively identifies him by name. Later, Ramesses II added a stone facing, with reliefs and inscriptions, to the south side of the temple's Second Pylon (below), and other Ramesside kings also decorated the side walls of the Second Court and added their names to the walls of the gate in the First Pylon. They do not seem, however, to have made major changes to the structure of the temple itself.

One of the few inscriptions remaining in the Mut Temple was carved on the outer face of the west wall in the rear of the temple. The fragmentary text is a theological treatise describing Amen-Re's creation of the world and of humanity. It was written by Ramessu-Meryatum, High Priest of Re in Heliopolis and the sixteenth son of Ramesses II and his most famous wife, Nefertari, whose cartouche appears in the inscription. Nefertari's tomb in the Valley of the Queens is one of the most beautiful in Egypt.

The Mut Temple in the Twenty-fifth Dynasty

The next major expansion of the Mut Temple took place during the Twenty-fifth Dynasty. Under King Taharqa, Montuemhat, fourth prophet of Amen, mayor of Thebes and governor of Upper Egypt, directed extensive work within the Mut Temple, rebuilding most of it using blocks from the earlier temple as building material. He also carried out a great deal of work elsewhere in the site. His most famous statue, shown above, was found by Benson and Gourlay and is one of the treasures of the Egyptian Museum, Cairo.

As a demonstration of the extent of his power, Montuemhat included a small chapel to himself within the east wall of the temple's Second Court that describes work he carried out in the Mut Precinct and other temples in Upper Egypt. Because the rear wall shows Taharqa; Montuemhat's father, Nesptah; Montuemhat; and his son (also named Nesptah) offering to Mut, it is known as the Montuemhat Crypt (or the Taharqa Crypt) even though it is actually a chapel. Private individuals, no matter how powerful, were not usually commemorated this way.

The texts and decoration of the crypt were copied by Mariette and appear in his 1875 book on Karnak. Using his own

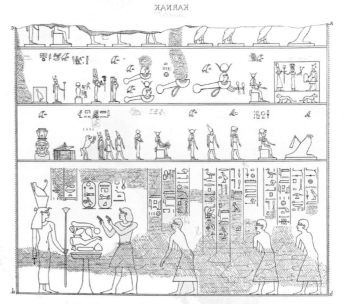

copy of Mariette's book, Charles Edwin Wilbour, an early American Egyptologist, corrected Mariette's drawings as in the scene on the rear wall. In the book, the texts are reversed; on the actual wall, Mut is on the left. They are shown here in their proper orientation. Wilbour's books form the core of the Brooklyn Museum's Wilbour Library of Egyptology, a superb research library.

The Contra-Temple

Montuemhat also built a small Contra-Temple abutting the rear wall of the Mut Temple. It was accessible only from the Isheru and perhaps from an ambulatory around the temple walls. The Contra-Temple was probably used in rituals celebrating the beginning of the inundation, symbolized by the return of the goddess from the south (see "Stories of Sekhmet," pages 8–9). What is left of its inscriptions duplicates some of the biographical texts from the Montuemhat Crypt. The entrance (above) bears an inscription by Nectanebo II, and the façade and a doorway between two rooms were decorated in the Ptolemaic Period, probably by Ptolemy VIII.

In the corridor to the east of the Contra-Temple, the Hopkins expedition built a small Open Air Museum to display and protect the superbly carved blocks from the early Hatshepsut/Thutmose III Mut Temple that had been reused in the foundations of the later temple.

Temple A

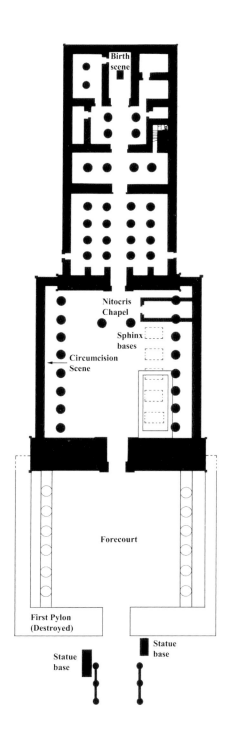

Birth scene

Nitocris Chapel

Sphinx bases

Circumcision Scene

Forecourt

First Pylon (Destroyed)

Statue base

Statue base

This temple stands in the northeast corner of the Precinct, at right angles to the Mut Temple. It is, in fact, larger than the Mut Temple and is the largest structure at the site. For much of its history Temple A stood outside the Mut Precinct (known as per-Mut or per-Isheru: "House of Mut" or "House of Isheru") in a separate place called Ipet. The photograph above indicates the approximate extent of the Mut Precinct throughout the New Kingdom and Temple A's relation to it. Amenhotep III may have built the original version of Temple A, but nothing of his remains and we have no idea what its name or purpose was at that time.

The first king who can definitely be associated with the temple is Ramesses II, by whose reign Temple A was a "temple of millions of years" dedicated to the king and to Amen-Re.

A doorjamb of Ramesses II's temple, found reused in later construction, provides part of the temple's name at that time: "Men-Ramesses-Akh-en-Amen..."

(Ramesses, who is beneficial to Amen...). It is the only indication of the temple's name at any period in its history.

The Forecourt and First Pylon

Ramesses II renovated and expanded the temple, adding a new Forecourt with a colonnade and a mud brick pylon (now completely gone), in front of which stood the two colossal statues and the Hittite Marriage stela found by Maurice Pillet (see page 17). Rather than commissioning new statues, Ramesses simply replaced the original owners' names with his own on existing statues. The head and one arm of the larger statue and the head of the smaller are in the British Museum and are clearly Amenhotep III. This kind of recycling was not uncommon in ancient

Egypt, but Ramesses II was a particularly notable usurper of his predecessors' monuments.

Sometime in the late Ptolemaic or the early Roman Period, the Forecourt ceased to have a ritual function and became instead an industrial area, with a kiln, what may have been a large well, and evidence of housing as well.

In 1979, the Brooklyn expedition discovered a second monumental alabaster stela to the south of the smaller colossal statue. This stela records Ramesses' work on a temple, most likely Temple A before which it stood. The stela was carved on a block from the same Amenhotep II shrine as the Hittite Marriage Stela (visible in the background) and both preserve wonderful early Eighteenth Dynasty reliefs.

Hittite Marriage Stela

**Rebuilt Amunhotep II Chapel
Karnak Open Air Museum**

Building Stela

Both stelae were removed to the Karnak Temple Open Air Museum in 2003, when the Amenhotep II shrine from which the slabs came was rebuilt.

All that is left of the First Pylon are its foundations and granite threshold. When turned over, one of the granite blocks proved to be the base of an over-life size statue of Nefertiti flanked by two of her daughters. Although no names are preserved, the style of the feet is unmistakably Amarna Period. The base is probably from a statue that once stood in Akhenaten's temple in East Karnak.

The First Court
Temple A remained outside the Mut Precinct, within its own enclosure walls, until the Twenty-fifth Dynasty, by which time it had become a mammisi or "birth house" where the birth of Mut's and Amen's divine child, Khonsu, was celebrated. Work in the rear of the temple probably began under Shabaka

(c. 705–690 BC), Taharqa's predecessor, but the bulk of the renovations took place during Taharqa's reign. Because he claimed to be a direct son of Amen, reliefs depicting Taharqa's divine conception and birth were carved onto the north wall of the temple's First Court (page 49). The most famous shows the circumcision of Taharqa and his royal *ka* (spirit/soul).

On the south side of the court the Brooklyn expedition has uncovered a series of stone rectangles that appear to be remains of a row of bases for sphinxes. The sphinxes were eventually removed and the bases incorporated into later constructions of the area. While the date is uncertain, these bases may represent a short sphinx avenue whose sculptures were removed when the temple was rebuilt, perhaps sometime during the Ramesside Period.

East of the sphinx bases, in the southeast corner of the court, the Brooklyn expedition uncovered the foundations of a small limestone chapel.

Lying nearby was the chapel's lintel depicting the God's Wife of Amen, Nitocris I (see page 39). It is shown below. While there are several chapels to God's Wives in the Amen Precinct and at Medinet Habu, it is most unusual to find one actually within a major temple.

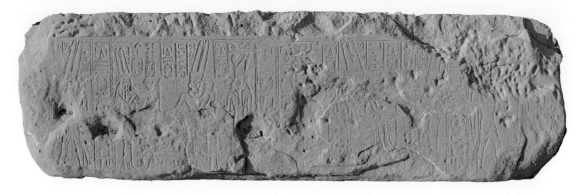

God's Wives were normally daughters or sisters of a king, and by the eighth century BC wielded considerable political power. These priestesses could even be shown performing rituals formerly reserved for kings, such as offering to the gods as Nitocris does on the chapel's lintel.

The Second Pylon

Taharqa also built (or rebuilt) Temple A's Second Pylon, whose north wing has a mud brick core with a sandstone facing. As the Brooklyn expedition discovered, the facing and the south wing (which seems to be solid stone) were partly constructed of broken-up statues (feet, torsos, heads) that once stood in the court of Ramesses III's temple. Reusing pieces of older, now less-used temples in the construction of new ones was not uncommon.

The front of the doorway in this pylon bears reliefs and inscriptions by Nectanebo I (above), one of the last native Egyptian pharaohs, but the reliefs on the reveals of the doorway (below) were carved in the Ptolemaic Period.

The Rear of the Temple

While Taharqa completed the renovation of Temple A, the raised reliefs in the rear of the temple are more characteristic of Shabaka's reign. However, the only direct evidence of Shaba-ka's presence in this part of the temple is a single block bearing a partially erased cartouche with his name.

The Central Sanctuary

A Ptolemaic relief of Mut, her divine child, and other gods on the rear wall of the central sanctuary shows that the temple remained a mammisi through the Ptolemaic Period and proba-bly until the end of its history as a religious monument.

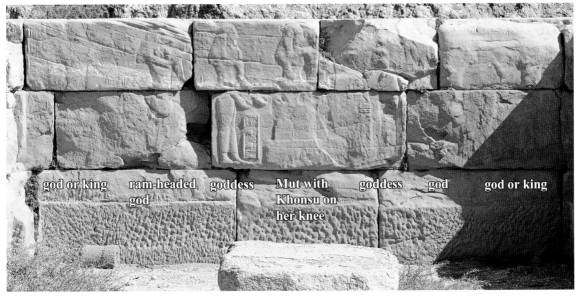

Chapel B

This building stands on a rise of ground south of Temple A and east of the Mut Temple. A paved roadway, of which portions remain, leads from the Mut Temple's First Court to the chapel, whose ancient name is not known. It may have been the place for the preparation of divine offerings mentioned in the Mut Temple's Montuemhat Crypt (see page 42) but was probably completely rebuilt by Nectanebo II in the Thirtieth Dynasty.

Very little of the structure remains beyond its mud brick foundations, the stone foundations and first course of the sanctuary (below), the foundations of parts of two doorways, the south wing of the gateway leading to the rear, and part of the roadway leading to the Mut Temple. The structure has never been excavated.

The Northwest Quadrant:
Taharqa Gate and
Ptolemaic Chapel

When Brooklyn began work in 1976, only a few small walls and some scattered blocks were visible in the northwest quadrant of the precinct. The inscriptions on the walls had been copied in the late 1800s by Wilbour (see page 43), who spent many years in Egypt studying the ancient monuments. Below is a page from his notebook showing one of the inscriptions and the wall as it is today. By the 1970s, the upper part of this wall had disappeared, so Wilbour's notes are the only record we have of its inscriptions.

King   Goddess

The Ptolemaic Chapel

The walls belong to a small chapel built by Ptolemy VI and Ptolemy VIII. Because its walls were in poor shape, the Brooklyn team dismantled the whole building and rebuilt it from the ground up.

The chapel's front room was dedicated to Mut and a lioness-headed goddess named Ash-Sedjmes, a protector of young women. This is one of the few reliefs of Mut preserved in her precinct. The rear room was probably dedicated to the Ptolemaic ancestor cult as the expedition found a block there showing Ptolemy VI worshiping two of his deified ancestors.

The Taharqa Gate

South and west of the Ptolemaic chapel the Brooklyn expedition discovered the top of a monumental gateway more than seven meters wide. No sign of it was visible on the surface and it did not appear on nineteenth-century maps of the site.

The gate and the wall into which it was set were built by Taharqa to enlarge the Mut Precinct and bring Temple A and the area north of the Mut Temple into the precinct, which until then extended no further north than the Mut Temple's First Pylon. The gate opened a new processional way to Temple A. The Ptolemaic chapel was later built just inside the north wing of the gateway.

The sandstone blocks of which the gate was built were in terrible condition (left), to the point that the gate was unstable. Thanks to the skill of the Egyptian conservators and stone masons who are part of the team (right), the Brooklyn expedition was able to dismantle the gate and not only rebuild it, but restore several fallen blocks to their original position.

West of the Taharqa Gate

The Taharqa Gate and its walls remained the western limit of the Mut Precinct for succeeding dynasties, probably to the time of the last native Egyptian pharaohs. However, when the new enclosure walls were built in the fourth century BC, the Taharqa Gate was no longer needed. It was eventually blocked and the land to the west was filled in and leveled so that houses could be built.

The houses stood within the protection of the new enclosure walls but outside the sacred area of the precinct, whose western limit probably remained the walls running off the Taharqa Gate. The village was occupied from about the late third century BC to the mid-second century AD, when the Mut Precinct went out of use as a religious center. Little remains of these buildings now but their mud brick foundations.

Temple of Ramesses III

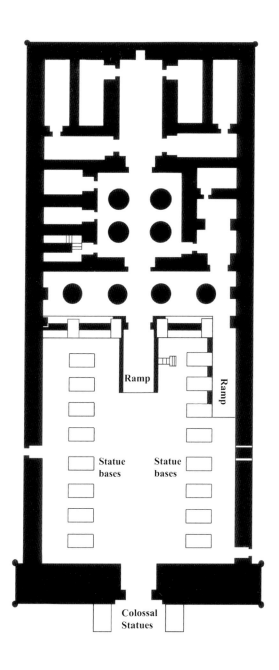

Ramp

Ramp

Statue
bases

Statue
bases

Colossal
Statues

This temple, at the southwest corner of the Isheru, was built around 1180 BC and appears to be dedicated to a creator form of the god Amen, a form associated with the god Min of Coptos who was always shown ithyphallic. A cult of Osiris seems also to have taken place in the temple. Very little is left of the interior except the bases of the statues that once lined the east and west sides of the First Court, the ramps between the court and the rear of the temple, and the lowest courses of the interior walls.

Like Temple A, the Ramesses III temple originally stood outside the Mut Precinct. The First Court seems to have been out of use by the Twenty-fifth Dynasty, when its statues were broken up to be used in building Temple A's Second Pylon (see page 51). The temple was brought into the precinct when the final enclosure walls were built in the fourth century BC, but how the temple functioned during the Ptolemaic and Roman Periods is unknown. The careful breaking up and burial of the cult statue (see page 68) under the paving suggests that some cultic activity continued there late into the precinct's history.

Pillet excavated the temple in the 1920s (see page 17) and re-erected the two colossal statues of the king before what is left of the temple's entrance.

The reliefs on the outside of the west wall show Ramesses III's campaigns against Syrians and Libyans. Most copy similar scenes at Medinet Habu and scenes of Ramesses II's battles on the walls of Karnak's Amen Temple. The most flagrant copy is about halfway along the west wall and reproduces Ramesses II's account of the battle at Kadesh.

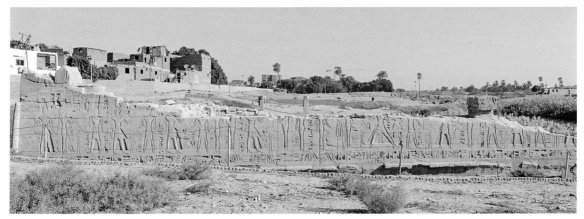

The reliefs on the south wall are traditional scenes showing Ramesses III offering to various gods, including the Theban Triad, and presenting them with prisoners and spoils of victory.

In 2002, the Hopkins expedition discovered a magnificent statue of Ramesses III, broken but nearly complete, in the rear of the temple. This statue, which was the temple's cult statue (the focus of the Temple's rituals), has been restored and is now on view in the Luxor Museum.

The Sacred Lake and the
South Half of the Precinct

The Sacred Lake (Isheru)

The Isheru is fed by underground springs leading from the Nile and rose and fell with the flooding of the Nile. The lake edge, at least that part surrounding the Mut Temple, was probably originally faced with stone and the lake was surely more regular in shape in antiquity. Once the site was abandoned and the lake edges no longer maintained, centuries of flooding eroded the shores, particularly on the west side.

As the relief in Khabekhenet's tomb (page 14) shows, the Isheru had two quays from which Mut's sacred barque could be launched to sail on the lake during religious ceremonies. The existing west quay, however, is much later in date.

The quay on the west arm of the lake has an earthen core with a stone facing. Most of the blocks are reused and date to the reign of Hakoris (c. 393–381 BC) of the Twenty-ninth Dynasty. Both Brooklyn and Hopkins excavated here and found no trace of a stone facing for the lake.

The quay on the east arm had become buried in dirt and debris from the reeds lining the lake. In 2009, the Hopkins expedition obtained a grant from ARCE to drain the lake (as part of the overall Karnak dewatering project sponsored by USAID) in order to investigate the lake edge. The expedition found that the east quay was preserved to a much greater height than the west quay and includes part of a long stone wall. The size of this structure suggests that it played some role in supporting the peninsula upon which the Mut temple was built.

South of the Sacred Lake

Excavations by the Hopkins expedition on the rise south of the Isheru revealed remains of very large granaries as well as bakeries and small workshops dating to the early Eighteenth Dynasty and attached to the Eighteenth Dynasty south enclosure wall. The circular granaries were enclosed by mud brick walls. The area was reused but not, apparently, rebuilt in the Twenty-fifth and Twenty-sixth Dynasties when the temple was actively renovated.

Below the Eighteenth Dynasty industrial installation, the Hopkins team came upon an unexpected find: a cemetery dating to the Seventeenth Dynasty or perhaps the very early Eighteenth Dynasty. The burials were a combination of poorer Egyptian ones with bodies placed on their backs in shallow graves scooped out of the earth, and Nubian-style tumulus graves with the occupants in the fetal position. In all cases the deceased were accompanied by very simple grave goods: pottery vessels, amulets, beads. It is quite clear that both sides of the enclosure at this date belonged to industrial elements of the Mut Temple. The cemetery at lower levels, dating to the late Second Intermediate Period, cannot be clearly associated with the temple, but the poverty of the burials suggests that these may have been people attached to the temple as serfs. The bones have been removed for study and the granaries and graves have all been reburied to preserve them.

Limited excavations by the Hopkins expedition in the large, flat area south of the Isheru have revealed remains of Late Period buildings, but not enough has been uncovered to determine their extent or purpose. It is entirely possible that this area was part of an administrative complex.

Chronology of Ancient Egyptian Dynasties

*Note: **All dates before 664 BC are approximate.***

Predynastic Period

Badarian Period (c. 4400–3800 BC)
Naqada I Period (c. 3800–3650 BC)
Naqada II Period (c. 3650–3300 BC)
Naqada III Period (c. 3300–3100 BC)
Dynasty 0 (c. 3100–3000 BC)

Early Dynastic Period

First Dynasty (c. 3000–2860 BC)
Second Dynasty (c. 2860–2686 BC)

Old Kingdom

Third Dynasty (c. 2686–2613 BC)
Fourth Dynasty (c. 2613–2494 BC)
Fifth Dynasty (c. 2494–2345 BC)
Sixth Dynasty (c. 2345–2181 BC)

First Intermediate Period

Seventh and Eighth Dynasties (c. 2181–2160 BC)
Ninth and Tenth Dynasties (c. 2160–2025 BC)
First half of the Eleventh Dynasty (c. 2125–2055 BC)

Middle Kingdom

Latter half of the Eleventh Dynasty (c. 2055–1985 BC)

Twelfth Dynasty (c. 1985–1773 BC)

Thirteenth Dynasty (c. 1773–after 1650 BC)

Fourteenth Dynasty (dates uncertain, contemporaneous with later Thirteenth Dynasty)

Second Intermediate Period

Fifteenth Dynasty (c. 1650–1550 BC) ("Hyksos" kings)

Sixteenth Dynasty (contemporaneous with Fifteenth Dynasty)

Seventeenth Dynasty (c. 1585–1550 BC)

New Kingdom

Eighteenth Dynasty (c. 1550–1295/92 BC)

Ahmose (or Amosis) (c. 1550–1525 BC)

Amenhotep (or Amenophis) I (c. 1525–1504 BC)

Thutmose (or Thutmosis) I (c. 1504–1492 BC)

Thutmose II (c. 1492–1479 BC)

Hatshepsut (Regnant Queen, c. 1478/72–1458 BC)

Thutmose III (c. 1479–1425 BC)

Amenhotep II (c. 1426–1400 BC)

Thutmose IV (c. 1400–1390 BC)

Amenhotep III (c. 1390–1353 BC)

Amenhotep IV, later called Akhenaten (c. 1353–1336 BC)

Nefernefruaten (c. 1336–1332 BC)

Smenkhkare (c. 1336–1332 BC)

Tutankhamen (c. 1332–1322 BC)

Ay (c. 1322–1319 BC)

Horemheb (c. 1319–1292 BC)

Nineteenth Dynasty (c. 1292–1190 BC)

Ramesses (or Ramses) I (c. 1292–1290 BC)

Sety (or Sethos) I (c. 1290–1279 BC)

Ramesses II (c. 1279–1213 BC)

Merneptah (c. 1213–1204 BC)

Sety II (c. 1204–1198 BC)

Amenmesse (c. 1203–1200 BC)

Siptah (c. 1198–1193 BC)

Tewosret (Regnant Queen, c. 1193–1190 BC)

Twentieth Dynasty (c. 1190–1075 BC)

Setnakhte (c. 1190–1187 BC)

Ramesses III (c. 1187–1156 BC)

Ramesses IV (c. 1156–1150 BC)

Ramesses V (c. 1150–1145 BC)

Ramesses VI (c. 1145–1137 BC)

Ramesses VII (c. 1137–1129 BC)

Ramesses VIII (c. 1128–1126 BC)

Ramesses IX (c. 1126–1108 BC)

Ramesses X (c. 1108–1104 BC)

Ramesses XI (c. 1104–1075 BC)

Third Intermediate Period

Twenty-first Dynasty ("Tanite") (c. 1075–945 BC)

Smendes (c. 1075–1049 BC)

Amenemnisu (c. 1049–1045 BC)

Psusennes I (c. 1045–997 BC)

Amenemope (c. 997–984 BC)

Osorkon the Elder (or Osochor) (c. 984–978 BC)

Siamun (c. 978–959 BC)

Psusennes II (c. 959–945 BC)

Twenty-Second Dynasty ("Bubastite") (c. 945–712 BC)

About ten rulers including:

Sheshenq I (c. 945–924 BC)

Osorkon II (c. 874–835/30 BC)

Sheshenq III (c. 835/30–783/78 BC)

Twenty-Third Dynasty (c. 838–712 BC)

Numerous rival rulers at Thebes and in the north of Egypt
including:

Pedubast I

Iuput I

Sheshenq IV

Osorkon III

Takeloth III

Rudamen

Iuput II

Sheshenq VI (?)

Twenty-fourth Dynasty ("Saite") (c. 727–712 BC)

Tefnakhte (c. 727–719 BC)

Bakenrenef (or Bocchoris) (c. 719–712 BC)

Twenty-fifth Dynasty ("Nubian" or "Kushite") (c. 760–656 BC)

Kashta (c. 760–747 BC)

Piye (or Piankhy) (c. 747–716 BC)

Shebitku (c. 716–705 BC)

Shabaka (c. 705–690 BC)

Taharqa (690–664 BC)

Tantamani (664–656 BC)

Late Period

Twenty-sixth Dynasty ("Saite") (664–525 BC)

Psamtik (or Psammetichus) I (664–610 BC)

Necho II (610–595 BC)

Psamtik II (595–589 BC)

Apries (589–570 BC)

Amasis (570–526 BC)

Psamtik III (526–525 BC)

Twenty-seventh Dynasty (First Persian Period: 525–404 BC)

Cambyses (525–522 BC)

Darius I (521–486 BC)

Xerxes I (485–465 BC)

Darius II (423–404 BC)

Twenty-eighth Dynasty (404–399 BC)
Amyrtaeus of Sais

Twenty-ninth Dynasty (399–380 BC)
Kings from Mendes:
Nepherites I (399–393 BC)
Hakoris (393–381 BC)
Nepherites II (381 BC)

Thirtieth Dynasty (381–343 BC)
Kings from Sebennytos:
Nectanebo I (381–362 BC)
Teos (365–362 BC)
Nectanebo II (362–343 BC)

Thirty-first Dynasty (Second Persian Period: 343–332 BC)
Three rulers including
Artaxerxes III Ochus (343–338 BC)
Darius III Codoman (335–332 BC)
Khababash (?), a native rebel ruler, may also belong to this
period

Macedonian and Ptolemaic Periods
Macedonian Dynasty (332–305 BC)
Alexander III, the Great (332–323 BC)
Philip III Arrhidaeus (323–317 BC)
Alexander IV (317–305 BC)

Ptolemaic Dynasty (305–30 BC)
Ptolemy I Soter I (323–282 BC: as "satrap" 323–305 BC; as king
of Egypt 305–282 BC)
Ptolemy II Philadelphos (285–246 BC)
Ptolemy III Euergetes I (246–222/1 BC)
Ptolemy IV Philopator (222/1–205 BC)

Ptolemy V Epiphanes (209/8–180 BC)

Ptolemy VI Philometor (180–164 BC, 163–145 BC)

Ptolemy VII Neos Philopator (145 BC)

Ptolemy VIII Euergetes II, or Physkon (170–163 BC, 145–116 BC)

Ptolemy IX Soter II, or Lathyros (116–110 BC, 109–107 BC, 88–80 BC)

Ptolemy X Alexander I (110–109 BC, 107–88 BC)

Ptolemy XI Alexander II (80 BC)

Ptolemy XII Neos Dionysos, or Auletes (80–58 BC, 55–51 BC)

Cleopatra VII Philopator (51–30 BC; initially with her brothers Ptolemy XIII and XIV)

Ptolemy XV Caesarion (45–30 BC)

Roman Period (30 BC–AD 337)

Egypt ruled by Roman emperors. Only emperors attested in the Mut Precinct by inscriptions or coins are listed

Octavian (later Augustus)	30 BC–AD 14
Tiberius	AD 14–37
Nero	AD 54–68
Trajan	AD 98–117
Hadrian	AD 117–138
Antoninus Pius	AD 138–161

Glossary

Amen

Egypt's imperial god, also known as Amen-Re when syncretized with the earlier sun god Re. His cult originated in Thebes, where he was one of the major gods, along with Montu, whose temple complex (North Karnak) lies to the north of the Amen Precinct at Karnak. Amen is normally shown as a human male, but can also appear as a ram, a ram-headed human, or with the head of a falcon as Amen-Re.

Barque Station

The special structure within a temple where the deity's sacred barque was stored when not needed for rituals.

Contra-Temple

A small temple built against the rear wall of a major temple. Contra-Temples were not accessible from within the temple itself. In the Mut Precinct, the Contra-Temple was built against the rear wall of the Mut Temple in the Twenty-fifth Dynasty and was accessible only from the Isheru and, perhaps, from an ambulatory around the outside of the temple.

Criosphinx

Sculpture of a recumbent ram, often with a figure of a king standing between the forelegs under the ram's chin. The ram usually represents Amen or Amen-Re in his ram form and symbolizes the god protecting the king.

Cult statue

The focus of the cults of Egyptian temples was a statue of the god housed in the temple's central shrine (the holy of holies). The statue would be ritually bathed and dressed daily and offerings presented to it. On festival days, the statue would be placed in its sacred barque and carried or sailed in processions to other temples.

Divine Triad

A group of three deities forming a divine family: usually a father god, mother goddess, and their divine son. The best-known divine family triad is that of Osiris, Isis, and Horus. In Thebes from the New Kingdom onward the major divine triad was Amen, Mut, and Khonsu. In Lower Egypt, the triad was Ptah, Sekhmet, and Nefertum.

Intermediate Period

Periods of political and/or economic instability during which control of the country was fragmented. The First Intermediate Period began with the collapse of the Old Kingdom. The Second Intermediate Period followed the Middle Kingdom and was a time when foreign kings known as the Hyksos ruled the northern half of the country. The Third Intermediate Period followed the New Kingdom and was characterized by rule by a number of foreign but Egyptianized kings of Libyan and Kushite (Sudanese) origin.

Isheru

Egyptian temples generally had a sacred lake in which rituals of purification and other rituals took place. Temples to Eye of Re goddesses had a specific form of sacred lake called an Isheru, of which the one at the Mut Precinct in South Karnak is the best preserved. These lakes wrapped around their temples, providing a safe haven in which the Eye of Re could give birth to her divine offspring.

Ithyphallic

With an erect penis symbolizing the god's generative powers; the normal way in which the god Min is portrayed, although other gods can also be shown ithyphallically.

Karnak

The complex of temples located in the ancient Upper Egyptian capital of Thebes (modern Luxor). It is made up of three major temple precincts: the Montu Precinct (North Karnak), the Amen Precinct (Karnak), and the Mut Precinct (South Karnak). The Amen Precinct also contains the temple of Khonsu.

Khonsu

The son of Amen and Mut, Khonsu is normally shown mummiform and wearing a headdress that includes both a crescent moon and a full moon.

Ptolemaic Period

Alexander the Great, a Macedonian Greek, conquered Nectanebo II, the last Egyptian pharaoh. On Alexander's death, control of his empire was split among his generals, with Ptolemy getting control of Egypt, first as satrap for Alexander's son and then for Alexander's brother, but from 305 BC as king in his own right. The Ptolemaic Dynasty (all of whose kings bore the name Ptolemy) ruled until 30 BC when Egypt, under Cleopatra VII, was conquered by the Romans.

Sacred barque

The boat in which the statue of the god was transported to other temples during festivals. As represented in reliefs, the prow and stern of the barque were adorned with images of the deity to whom the barque belonged. Barques could be carried by priests in processions or sailed on their deity's sacred lake or across the Nile as needed. When not in use, the boats were stored in a special structure within the temple called a barque station.

Further Reading

M. Benson and J. Gourlay, *The Temple of Mut in Asher: An account of the Excavation of the Temple and of the Religious Representations and Objects Found Therein, as Illustrating the History of Egypt and the Main Religious Ideas of the Egyptians* (London, 1899)

B. Bryan, "Amunhotep III's Legacy in the Temple of Mut," in S. D'Auria (ed.), *Offerings to the Discerning Eye: An Egyptological Medley in Honor of Jack A. Josephson*, CHANE 38 (Leiden and Boston, 2010), 63–72

B. Bryan, "Hatshepsut and Cultic Revelries in the New Kingdom," in J. Balán, B. Bryan, P. Dorman (eds.), *Creativity and Innovation in the Reign of Hatshepsut. Occasional Proceedings of the Theban Workshop*, SAOC 69 (Chicago, 2014), 93–124

B. Bryan, "A Newly Discovered Statue of a Queen from the Reign of Amunhotep III," in S. D'Auria (ed.), *Servant of Mut: Studies in Honor of Richard A. Fazzini* (Leiden and Boston, 2008), 32–43

The Epigraphic Survey, *Reliefs and Inscriptions at Karnak* II, *Ramses III's Temple Within the Great Enclosure of Amun, Part II, and Ramses III's Temple in the Precinct of Mut*, OIP 35 (Chicago, 1936)

R. Fazzini, "Aspects of the Mut Temple's Contra-Temple at South Karnak Part II," in S. D'Auria (ed.), *Offerings to the Discerning Eye: An Egyptological Medley in Honor of Jack A. Josephson*, CHANE 38 (Leiden and Boston, 2010), 83–101

R. Fazzini, "A Monument in the Precinct of Mut with the Name of the God's Wife Nitocris I," H. De Meulenaere et al., *Artibus Aegypti. Studia in Honorem Bernardi V. Bothmer a Collegis, Amicis, Discipulis Conscripta* (Brussels, 1983), 51–62

R. Fazzini, "A Sculpture of King Taharqa (?) in the Precinct of the Goddess Mut at South Karnak," *Mélanges Gamal Eddin Mokhtar* I, BdÉ 97, 1 (Cairo, 1985), 293–306

R. Fazzini, "Some Aspects of the Precinct of the Goddess Mut in the New Kingdom," in E. Ehrenberg (ed.), *Leaving No Stones Unturned. Essays on the Ancient Near East and Egypt in Honor of Donald P. Hansen* (Winona Lake, Indiana, 2002), 63–76

R. Fazzini, "Two Semi-Erased Kushite Cartouches in the Precinct of Mut at South Karnak," in P. Brand and L. Cooper (eds.), *Causing His Name to Live: Studies in Egyptian Epigraphy and History in Memory of William J. Murnane*, CHANE 37 (Leiden, 2009), 95–101

R. Fazzini and P. O'Rourke, "Aspects of the Mut Temple's Contra-Temple at South Karnak—Part I", in L. Gabolde (ed.), *Hommages offerts à Jean-Claude Goyon pour son 70e anniversaire*, BdÉ 143 (2008), 139–50

R. Fazzini and J. van Dijk (eds.), *The First Pylon of the Mut Temple, South Karnak: Architecture, Decoration, Inscriptions* (Leuven, 2015)

S. Sauneron et al., *La porte ptolémaïque de l'enceinte de Mout à Karnak*, MIFAO 107 (Cairo, 1983)

J. van Dijk, "A Colossal Statue Base of Nefertiti and Other Early Atenist Monuments from the Precinct of the Goddess Mut in Karnak", in S. D'Auria (ed.), *Servant of Mut: Studies in Honor of Richard A. Fazzini* (Leiden and Boston, 2008), 246–61

E. Waraksa, *Female Figurines from the Mut Precinct: Context and Ritual Function* (Fribourg and Göttingen, 2007)

In addition, a history of the site and the reports on the Brooklyn Museum's seasons of fieldwork from 1996 onward are available online at www.brooklynmuseum.org/features/mut

For a yearly "dig diary" of the Johns Hopkins University expedition from 2001 to 2015, see "Hopkins in Egypt Today": http://pages.jh.edu/~egypttoday (cited March 2020)

Acknowledgments

Brooklyn Museum Expedition to the Mut Precinct, South Karnak

Director: Richard A. Fazzini, Curator Emeritus, Brooklyn Museum
The work of the Brooklyn Museum's archaeological expedition to the Precinct of Mut, South Karnak has been made possible by the generosity of a number of corporations, foundations, and individuals. The 1976–79 seasons were funded primarily by the Coca-Cola Company of Atlanta, Georgia. Institutional funding for subsequent seasons has been provided by the Brooklyn Museum's Charles Edwin Wilbour Fund and the Egyptian Art Council; The Founders Society and the Antiquaries of the Detroit Institute of Arts, the Samuel H. Kress Foundation, and the Long Island Society of the Archaeological Institute of America. Additional corporate support has come from Conoco, Inc.; the Getty Oil Company; American Motors, Inc.; and the Cairo Sheraton Hotel, Towers, and Casino. Major funding was also provided by the following individuals, listed in alphabetical order: Kitty Brush; Richard Fazzini and Mary McKercher; Marjorie Fisher; Louis D. Fontana; W. Benson Harer, Jr.; Jo Ann Harris; Jack Josephson and Magda Saleh; John Moran; William and Elsie Peck; Harold D. Winters; Beverly Zweiman. In addition, the following people have also con-

tributed to the work over the years: Heide van Doren Betz, Adelaide De Menil, James L. Frey, Howard Gilman, Theodore Halkedis, Charles Herzer and Adrienne Rourke, Mr. and Mrs. Sydney Jacoff, Reuben and Norma Kershaw, Alan May, Mrs. Henry L. Moses, Kathy Putnam, Carl and Florence Selden, Emma Swann Hall, and an anonymous Dutch donor. We thank them all for their generosity.

Johns Hopkins University Expedition to the Mut Precinct, South Karnak
Director: Betsy M. Bryan, Alexander Badawy Professor of Egyptian Art and Archaeology, The Johns Hopkins University
The Johns Hopkins University expedition acknowledges with thanks the generosity of Marjorie Fisher. It has also benefited from grants by the Egyptian Antiquities Project and the Egyptian Antiquities Conservation program of the American Research Center in Egypt.

Opening the Precinct to the Public
Both expeditions gratefully acknowledge the work of the American Research Center in Egypt's Luxor office, headed by John Shearman, in preparing the site to be opened to the public in January 2014. The work was supported by a grant from the United States Agency for International Development.

Photography Credits

pp. 35 (top), 37, 39 (right), 46, 55, 69, 72, 73: J. van Rensselaer IV for the Johns Hopkins University Expedition

pp. 14, 18, 22 (top), 26 (top), 32 (top), 58 (top), 59 (top), 61 (top), 63: D. Loggie for the Brooklyn Museum Mut Expedition

page 16 (top): unknown; (bottom): M. Benson, J. Gourlay, *The Temple of Mut in Asher* (London, 1899), pl. 5

page 17: (top): Collection M. Pillet, CNRS-MOM, année 1921, inv. B137-10; copyright CNRS-MOM; (bottom): Collection M. Pillet, CNRS-MOM, année 1921, inv. B134-10; copyright CNRS-MOM

pp. 7 (right), 33 (left), 41 (top), 57: J. van Dijk for the Brooklyn Museum Mut Expedition

pp. 39 (top) JE31886c,d; (right) JE99281; 41 (bottom) CG647: illustrated courtesy of the Egyptian Museum, Cairo

pp. 12, 68 (top): illustrated courtesy of the Luxor Museum, Luxor

All other photographs: M. McKercher for the Brooklyn Museum Mut Expedition

Maps, Line Drawings
Plans on pp. 25, 35, 45: W.H. Peck for the Brooklyn Museum Mut Expedition

page 15: *Description de l'Egypte. Antiquités*, vol. 3 (2nd edition 1821–30), pl. 16 (top). Brooklyn Museum Libraries. The Wilbour Library of Egyptology, Special Collections

page 15 (bottom), 42 (bottom): A. Mariette, *Karnak, étude topographique et archéologique* (Leipzig, 1875), pls. 3, 43 with annotations by Charles Edwin Wilbour. Brooklyn Museum Libraries. The Wilbour Library of Egyptology, Special Collections

page 58 (center): Brooklyn Museum Archives, Wilbour Archival Collection, Notebooks [5.1.007]: 2G (04/05/1884–04/07/1886)

Index